DURANGO
SECOND EDITION

The Strater Hotel circa 1897 – courtesy of the Animas Museum

DURANGO

SECOND EDITION

BY MAUREEN KEILTY

PHOTOGRAPHY BY DAN PEHA

SunDagger

INCORPORATED

DURANGO, COLORADO

Also by Maureen Keilty

Best Hikes with Children in Colorado · Mountaineers Books, 1991, 1998
Best Hikes with Children in Utah · Mountaineers Books, 1993

For Paul – for making it happen.

Second Edition, 1998 by Sun Dagger, Inc.
Post Office Box 93 · Durango, Colorado 81302 · 970/259-3933

Book Design by Paul Ambrose

Printed in the United States of America
by Pyramid Printing, Grand Junction, Colorado

Library of Congress Catalog Card Number: 98-86685

ISBN 0-9665878-3-9

CONTENTS

ACKNOWLEDGMENTS

In addition to the people who assisted us in creating the first addition of DURANGO, we thank the following people and businesses for their guidance and verifications on this second edition project: Robert McDaniel, *La Plata County Historical Society*; Christy Nelson and Jeff Jackson, *D&SNGRR*; Patty Zink, *Durango Area Chamber Resort Association*; Kathy Metz, *Durango Parks & Recreation*; Sharon Hatch, Michael Burke, *U.S. Forest Service, Columbine Ranger District*; Mike Japhet and Barb Horn, *Colorado Division of Wildlife*; Andy Gleason and Doug Lewis, *Lead Avalanche Forecasters*; Linda Towle, *Mesa Verde National Park*; Mike Smedley, *Purgatory Ski Area*; Nancy Wiley, *Four Corners River Sports*; Dave Grossman, *Duranglers*; John Glover, *Outdoorsman*; Casey Lynch, *Mountain Waters Rafting*, Rebecca Hershman and Chris Fickle, rockclimbers. The use of historic photos by the La Plata County Historical Society, Fort Lewis College Center for Southwest Studies, and Trimble Hot Springs. Many thanks to Ruth Cross for her patient and thorough editing skills. Special thanks to Niko for his antics and laughter when we needed it most.

Approaching Paradise

Nestled comfortably in the Animas Valley, with its mountainous entry at the north end and doorway to the desert Southwest at the other, Durango is a desirable destination. Its earliest occupants, the Ancestral Puebloans of nearly 2,500 years ago, flourished here and took full advantage of the abundant wildlife and ideal growing conditions. It was a time and place described as "a close approach to paradise" by archaeologist Earl Morris. Centuries later, Ute Indians hunted and fished the region and may have settled temporarily in the simple cave structures left by the earliest inhabitants.

In 1860, a prospector probing the San Juan Mountains north of Durango discovered flakes of gold, triggering a flood of people – treasure hunters eager to strike paydirt, be it gold or silver. Their entry drew the railroad industry to Durango, and its legacy remains a key attraction.

Today, the same natural elements that originally brought people to the area continue to do so. The Animas River, once essential as a food and water source, is now a premier recreation site that lures boaters and anglers. The surrounding two million acres of San Juan National Forest, where once hunter-gatherers roved and later miners probed, now establishes Durango as headquarters for skiers, hunters, hikers, bikers, climbers and an untold number of outdoor enthusiasts. Artists, both performing and graphic, inspired by the area's unmatched splendor settle here. And those seeking refuge from city strife find Durango's small-town ambience coupled with spectacular scenery the answer to their search.

Durango's ever-increasing number of residents compose a varied lot. Yet, a cooperative spirit called volunteerism unites them. It is the force behind such international events as the Iron Horse Bicycle Classic or the care behind such local needs as the Area Agency on Aging. Volunteers are the tutors for the Adult Learning Center, the extended family for the Family Center and the instructors for the Adaptive Sports Association. They are the actors who present plays, display art and bring internationally known musicians to town. Members of more than 80 civic organizations provide the people-helping-people support that makes Durango a caring community. It is this theme of shared responsibility that will protect Durango's natural assets. It is clear, however, that the region's growing population is being tested – challenged to preserve the landscape yet plan for increased housing and commercial development. No easy solutions exist. Durango's future requires careful choices; those that achieve "a close approach to paradise" are what everyone wants.

The Strater Hotel, Durango's elegant landmark since 1887

"A New Wonder of the Southwest"

Long before a surveyor's stake established Durango in 1880, human habitation here was periodic. Beginning around 300 B.C., Ancestral Puebloans occupied the region in rock shelters and pithouses for a thousand years. Later, Ute, Navajo and Pueblo clans lived in the Animas Valley, though briefly, as did Spaniards in search of gold and the occasional trapper seeking beaver in the mountain streams.

Unidentified Ute Indian
Animas Museum

While Civil War gunpowder still darkened the skies of eastern states, prospectors began finding their way to the Animas Valley. However, isolation and the threat of trespassing on Indian land shortened their stay. By the 1870s, prospectors, merchants, farmers and families started establishing homes in the valley, deriving their livelihood by furnishing the area's mining camps with farm products and other necessities. In its first year, Durango boasted 2,500 residents, 134 businesses including an array of saloons, several newspapers, doctors, lawyers and one church.

Following the rural pioneers, a core of progressive, independent urban entrepreneurs arrived, intent on carving out an economic empire not only in Durango but also in the San Juan Basin. Opening the region's economic avenues, the Denver and Rio Grande Railroad built the San Juan Extension from Durango to Silverton. Meanwhile, Otto Mears developed a network of roads that traversed southwestern Colorado.

Coal mining and smelting, at one time the town's biggest industry, thrived under the leadership of John Porter. Banking flourished under the direction of Ohioan Alfred Camp. Peter Fassbinder brought real estate to a profitable level. Charles Newman, a local druggist who later made a fortune with a Rico mine, underwrote construction of the Newman Block, much of which now stands at the corner of Eighth Street and Main Avenue. Thomas Graden not only established the flour and saw mills in town but also organized the Graden Mercantile Company. Destroyed by fire in 1948, Graden's half-block long building on Main Avenue's west side was rebuilt and now houses several shops and offices.

Alfred Camp established a banking dynasty in Durango in the late 1870s. His family's influence continued up until the 1960s.
Fort Lewis College Center for Southwest Studies

Entrepreneur Peter Fassbinder brought the first subdivision to Durango, spanning land north of 12th Street to the river. In order to sell his lots on the east side of the river, he built the first bridge over the Animas, only to watch an April flood wash it away.
Fort Lewis College Center for Southwest Studies

As the editor of the daily newspaper, the *Durango Record*, Caroline Wescott Romney was an outspoken patriot. Fearless and freewheeling with her journalism, she championed Durango as "the new wonder of the Southwest." She rallied for women's right to vote, and her newspaper called for Durango's only lacking resource, "those potent civilizers of their pioneer brothers – girls."

Meanwhile, the women of Durango, restricted to school and church outlets, determinedly backed town

Buckskin Charlie and pilot Walter Ansey step aboard an early bi-plane. As the chosen Ute leader by his noted predecessor Chief Ouray, Charlie was well respected for his ability to embrace Ute life fully yet absorb the best values of the white culture. He was a friend of Theodore Roosevelt and a Ute leader who insisted that all tribal ceremonies and crafts be carried out in the traditional manner.
Animas Museum

improvements. Their causes included abolition of the redlight district, Sunday business closings, music festivals, and the organized battle against the "drunken husband" corruption.

The San Juan Express stopped at the Durango station. It was the last regularly scheduled narrow gauge passenger train with service to Chama and Alamosa, circa 1940.
Animas Museum

Chief Ignacio led the Weenuche band of Utes during its difficult transition period adapting to reservation life beginning in the 1870s.
Animas Museum

On par with the times, racial discrimination had become well established in Durango. Mexican Americans found themselves relegated to the south side of town or across the tracks. Only a few African Americans lived in La Plata County, and these were restricted to the menial work of porters or cleaners. Likewise, Chinese residents were consigned to kitchen, laundry and gardening work. Ute Indians were not welcome in Durango except to trade or on their ration day when merchants anticipated increased sales.

Baseball was Durango's most popular sport in the early 1900s.
Animas Museum

Despite the disastrous downtown fire of 1889, Durango prospered until the silver crash of 1893.

Bubble blowers enjoy good, clean Victorian fun in one of Durango's Third Avenue homes. Note the refreshment containers.
Animas Museum

Then its smelter, fueled by locally mined coal, kept the town economically stable as did the railroads, the Denver & Rio Grande to Silverton and Otto Mear's Rio Grande Southern to the mining districts of Rico and Telluride. Agricultural pursuits kept many locals afloat during the decades between the wars.

With the start of World War II, Durango's smelter became a leading uranium concentrate producer, employing hundreds. Oil and gas development followed an up-and-down course becoming the economic mainstay it is today. By the time Durango reached 90 years of age, tourism was thriving while Fort Lewis College was expanding and home construction was on the rise.

Huck Finn look-alike catches a winner during Huck Finn days, c.1950.
Animas Museum

Today, many of Main Avenue's historic buildings remain. Many house art galleries and restaurants that provide yet another lure in promoting Durango as a tourist destination. A few industries have settled here utilizing "Made in Durango" as a marketing tool. The town receives world-wide recognition for its bicycling

Durango's original kayaker?
Animas Museum

and whitewater events that in turn create as much as 100,000 visitors annually in Durango. Train riders and skiers account for another major slice of the tourist pie feeding Durango's economy. Such popularity has taken its toll. The greed for profit in real estate continues to threaten Durango's small town heritage. As La Plata County's open space is diminished by subdivisions, more and more citizen groups are calling for city and county plans that accommodate growth while honoring the very essence of Durango's natural beauty. At this pivotal point in Durango's history, some say its destiny may be that of neighboring Telluride or Aspen. Still, it's the lessons learned by the newcomers and the values held by the natives that will determine the next chapter in Durango's story.

A WELL-WATERED PLACE
An Historic Time Line

■ 1860- Lured by Colorado's first gold strike, prospector Charles Baker leads a group into the valley where Silverton now sits. The group panned enough gold dust to spark the eventual flood of miners to the region.

■ 1870s- Settlers begin arriving in the Animas Valley, now the north part of Durango. Silverton's mining camps serve as a thriving market for their farm products and staples. Winter months bring many a bone-weary miner to be soothed in the nearby hot springs.

■ 1874- Ute Indians cede much of the San Juan Mountains in the Brunot Agreement, thus opening the region up to miners.

■ 1876- Animas City officially surveyed; two years later residents vote to incorporate.

■ 1879-80- Colorado's "baby railroad," the Denver & Rio Grande announces plans to lay narrow gauge track up the Animas Valley to Silverton. Negotiations between the

Ouray was chief of the Uncompahgre band of Utes that roamed the regions of the Gunnison and Uncompahgre rivers. Known as the chief of all the Utes, he was the primary negotiator for the 1873 Brunot Agreement that ceded most of the San Juan Mountains to the U.S Government and created the Ute reservations.
Animas Museum

town officials and the Denver & Rio Grande fail, leading the way to the formation of a new town, just two miles south – Durango.

Durango's first marshall, Robert Dwyer. His career lasted but one year when his deputy accidentally shot him. The serious wound in his neck forced him to turn to ranching.
Animas Museum

■ 1880- September 13, Durango's first survey stake is driven. Former territorial governor and D&RG negotiator A. C. Hunt names the town "Durango," possibly due to its similarity to Durango, Mexico, where he had traveled on railroad business. The name is a Spanish word meaning "well-watered place" or water town.

■ 1880- Metallurgist John Porter begins moving Silverton's smelter to the west bank of Durango's Animas River, to an area now called Smelter Mountain.

■ 1880- Plans drawn for Durango include a Main Avenue that would be a "wholesale street", Second Avenue, a "retail street", and Third Avenue, a residential boulevard with "rows of trees down the middle".

■ 1881- January 29, Durango's first hold-up is described in the Durango Record as a "sure sign of a booming town." Crime increases during the town's first

few months from petty theft and burglaries to two murders (the culprits were "jerked to Jesus"), followed by a shootout between opposing cattle gangs. Pioneer druggist John Taylor is elected Durango's first mayor, and a host of city offices and ordinances is prescribed.

■ 1881- December, City government attempts zoning by designating the red-light district to an area west of the railroad tracks downtown.

■ 1882- August D&RG reaches Silverton. Trimble Hot Spring's first hotel is built, a handsome two-story 6,500-square-foot building.

■ 1888- August, Durango's finest Victorian building, the Strater Hotel, opens "strictly first class in all appointments."

■ 1888- December, Richard Wetherill and brother-in-law Charlie Mason discover Cliff Palace at Mesa Verde, the largest cliff dwelling in North America.

■ 1889- Fire ravages seven blocks of businesses, residences and churches. Townspeople rebound, building the new structures using stone and bricks as originally recommended by the Durango Trust.

■ 1891- "Pathfinder of the San Juans," Otto Mears completes the 172-mile Rio Grande-Southern Railroad line that ran from Durango to Ridgway via Mancos, Dolores, Rico and Telluride, thereby providing direct connections with important mining districts in the San Juan Mountains.

■ 1891- Gustav Nordenskiold, Swedish archaeologist, makes the first scientific observations at Mesa Verde.

■ 1893- Sherman Silver Purchase Act is repealled thus collapsing the price of silver and closing mines in the San Juan Mountains. Durango's smelter closes, increasing unemployment during the century's worst depression.

■ 1893- Women's suffrage voted down in La Plata County, but Colorado approves women's right to vote.

■ 1894- Coal miners strike, demanding safety legislation, regular payment of wages and an end to the scrip system (company store credit).

■ 1895- Congress passes a bill giving Ute Indians the right to choose allotments of land, freeing more reservation land for white settlement.

■ 1901- Drought reduces the Animas River to a collection of puddles.

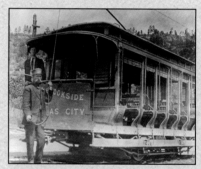

Motorman Joe McKenny poses in front of the summer rolling stock of the Durango Railway & Realty Company parked at the Animas City terminus.
Animas Museum

■ 1906- Mesa Verde is established as a national park due to the work of a Durango women's group.

■ 1907- La Plata County coal mining reaches an all-time record, nearly 2 percent of Colorado's yearly total.

■ 1911- Floodwaters wash out the D&RG's Animas Canyon tracks and rise 4 feet high on some of Durango's streets.

■ 1917- Wooden city sidewalks, a dry refuge from the street's knee-deep mud,

D&RG bridge east of the current Main Avenue bridge appears floating in the Animas River's floodwaters of 1911, the worst recorded flood to date. *Animas Museum*

are slowly replaced with cement. Tight city funds prohibit the paving of the streets.

■ 1918- Spanish flu epidemic strikes, closing the schools and businesses. People arriving via trains from other towns are placed under quarantine.

■ 1925- The Durango Exchange, later known as the Durango Chamber of Commerce, begins promoting the town as the "complete vacationland." With all roads and railroads leading to it, Durango becomes the key link to Mesa Verde.

■ 1925- Ku Klux Klan influence in Durango reaches its height when mostly Catholics and Mexicans are targeted. Klan membership draws from all classes; after a Klan rally weekend, those with clotheslines holding extra sheets are likely KKK members.

■ 1929- Durango's first municipal airport opens with a crash landing of a Douglas bomber. No one is injured. Depression delays daily service to Denver.

■ 1931- Zeke Flora, self-taught archaeologist, uncovers 19 mummified human remains in the Animas Valley's Falls Creek area, considered the oldest Ancient Pueblo site in the Southwest.

■ 1933- Works Progress Administration funds numerous Durango and La Plata County projects including the county fairgrounds on Main Avenue, its horse barns, grandstand and caretaker's house. Four years later, WPA funds go the the construction of Smiley Junior High School.

■ 1934- Noted archaeologist Earl Morris leads Mesa Verde's first permanent stabilization team. Their preservation work serves as a model for future projects.

■ 1935- Will Rogers, along with his wife and famous pilot Wiley Post, land in Durango and stay at the Strater Hotel. "Out of the way and glad of it" is Roger's parting assessment of Durango.

■ 1936- KIUP, Durango's first radio station, begins broadcasting.

■ 1941- Vallecito Dam is dedicated, a $3,300,000 project epitomizing the New Deal.

■ 1943- Durango's mill reprocesses vanadium tailings for uranium, vital to the Manhattan Project's atomic bomb development. Uranium milling becomes Durango's largest employer, aiding the post-war boom.

■ 1950s- La Plata County leads the state in natural gas production. Assessed property values triple, and the city's population increases 41 percent to 10,531.

■ 1951- Passenger service between Durango and Alamosa, the last regularly scheduled narrow gauge passenger train is canceled. The Durango to Silverton route continues with its seasonal schedule.

■ 1957- Fort Lewis College opens in Durango. Five years later, it becomes a

"Cowgirls on Parade" along Main Avenue. Smoke from the smelter drifts south of the Strater Hotel. *Animas Museum*

four-year, degree-granting school.

■ 1965- Purgatory Ski Area opens.

■ 1967- National Park Service recognizes the Durango to Silverton line as a National Historic Landmark.

■ 1974- Fire in the 800 block of Main destroys several buildings, later replaced by the Durango Mall.

■ 1981- Durango & Rio Grande sells its Durango to Silverton narrow gauge line to Charles Bradshaw, a Florida businessman, who commits to improving the line's service while preserving its 19th century charm.

■ 1989- February 10, Fire in the Durango roundhouse destroys the 1882 structure in which six vintage locomotives are badly damaged. The roundhouse and trains are rebuilt accurately according to historic records.

■ 1990- Name-brand factory outlet stores begin influx on Main Avenue.

■ 1992- Surge of new residents increases pressure on housing. Locals demand county zoning regulations as housing development threatens open space.

■ 1993- January 19, Fine Arts Auditorium at Fort Lewis College collapses under the weight of 52 inches of snow in two weeks. Season snowfall reaches a record 129 inches.

■ 1994- July 13-20, Dry conditions precede Black Ridge fire that burns 13,955 acres of private, unincorporated and Bureau of Indian Affairs land southwest of Durango.

■ 1997- The 612-seat Community Concert Hall at FLC opens as the first building in the three-part Cultural Arts Complex of Southwest Colorado.

■ 1998- Construction of a Wal-Mart superstore establishes Durango's southern corridor as a commercial and business district.

■ For a sampling of Durango's historic past, visit the Animas Museum on 31st Street and West Second Avenue.

Early engine of the Denver & Rio Grande

Photo courtesy of Fort Lewis College, Center for Southwest Studies

●

During a "run-by" the Fall Photographers' Train poses for the cameras.

A CENTURY OF STEAM

When the first passenger train steamed into Durango on August 1, 1881, the town declared itself united "by a band of steel to the civilized world." Indeed, just one year later a bold woman purchased a ticket at Durango's Denver and Rio Grande Railway office direct to Liverpool, England. Today, nearly 200,000 passengers a year step aboard the century-old, refurbished train at the Durango depot. Here they begin a ride unequaled in scenic splendor through the San Juan Mountains and the Animas River Valley to Silverton, an authentic Victorian mining town nearly 3,000 feet higher and 45 miles north of Durango.

"Silver by the ton" was the original incentive for the D&RG Railroad to lay tracks in southwestern Colorado. Silverton hosted dozens of mining camps after the Ute Indians signed the Brunot Agreement of 1873, forfeiting their rights to the surrounding mountains. The town remained isolated, dependent on packers and teamsters to haul supplies in and carry ore out over the rugged Continental Divide. Responding to and capitalizing on Silverton's predicament, D&RG Railroad laid track west from its north-south charter to El Paso, Texas.

Constructed at a feverish pace, the D&RG tracks reached Durango by way of Cumbres Pass, New Mexico, in time for the town's August 5, 1881, celebration. One week later, crews began laying tracks to Rockwood, a short-lived commmunity north of Durango that served as a railroad hub. From here, wagons and stagecoaches followed the toll road north to Silverton and west to Rico. Rockwood's vitality lasted just nine years. In 1891, the Rio Grande Southern Railroad reached Rico, over 100 rail miles north of Durango, thus eliminating Rockwood's primary function.

Throughout the winter and spring of 1881-82, a work crew of up to 850 men blasted a path along the Animas Gorge's near-vertical cliffs and constructed bridges across raging torrents, reaching Silverton in July 1882. This engineering feat was recognized in 1968 as a National Historic Civil Engineering Landmark by the American Society of Engineers.

Rock and mud slides, avalanches and floods have temporarily stopped the train in its trips to Silverton. Even the Roundhouse Fire of February 10, 1989, that destroyed most of the structure and badly damaged the six locomotives it contained, didn't prevent the train from blowing its start-up whistle on opening day that year. Today, the D&SNGRR remains the only regulated (by the Colorado Public Utilities Commission) 100 percent coal-fired narrow gauge railroad in the United States.

Full Steam Ahead

There's magic in a ride aboard the D&SNGRR. For some, it's hearing the whistles of the morning trains, signaling their moves, speaking a language only railroaders understand. Others are awed by the black smoke billowing from the stack, a vaporous suggestion of the coal-fired engine's power, enough to haul the 150-ton engine and 14 coaches with its 600 passengers up 3,000 feet to Silverton. The rails, set 3 feet apart as opposed to the standard 4 feet 8-1/2 inches, intrigue some. Narrow gauge, as it is called, allows the massive black locomotive to hug the granite mountain as it climbs impossible grades along its 45-mile journey.

Others relive history by riding the open gondola car, just as the miners did more than a century ago, feeling cinders dust their cheeks, watching for mine sites tucked in the mountain crevices. For many, the ride offers a privileged passage through one of the most stunning portions of the San Juan National Forest's two million acres. While traveling the heart of a dark spruce forest, they catch glimpses of jagged peaks draped with snow. Or as the train edges a granite cliff, they look down to the Animas River, rushing over boulders 400 feet below.

For most passengers on the D&SNGRR, the train's gentle side-to-side sway and rhythmic clicking transports them to another place, another time, allowing fond memories to fill their day.

Maintaining a history of uninterrupted service, the D&SNGRR provides several trips daily to Silverton from May through October. Leaving Durango in the morning, the three-hour, one-way trip makes few stops along its northward climb. The water towers at Tank Creek and Needleton refill the train's water tanks, located in the tender, with up to 5,000 gallons of water. Farther up it may halt for guests at Tall Timber resort or backpackers at Elk Park and Needleton,

A fireman shovels nearly four tons of coal into the firebox on a D&SNGRR steam locomotive enroute to Silverton. The engine consumes about one ton on its return trip to Durango.

where trailheads lead to the Weminuche Wilderness. During stops, passengers enjoy rail-side views of wildflowers carpeting meadows or a wall of mineralized rock once coveted by miners. The two-hour lunch-break in Silverton allows time for browsing through the numerous shops along the dirt streets of the old mining town. On the return route, those not lulled to sleep by the train's rhythmic swaying watch for different views of the mountains and river gorge.

Elegant private coaches are available for charter. The Nomad and the Cinco provide an antique velvet-curtained atmosphere for parties of 18 and 25 respectively. As the last car on the train, the Alamosa parlor car features the best views while offering adults a full bar in a club car setting. The Railcamp, a narrow-gauge boxcar refurbished as a recreational vehicle, serves as home for small groups wanting a comfortable stay in the San Juan Mountains. Passengers in wheelchairs ride The Home Ranch car equipped with a lift and adequate space for unrestricted movement.

Visitors to the D&SNGRR Museum, located in the train yard's original roundhouse, sample turn-of-the-century locomotive life. For some, watching the massive wood and iron turntable rotate an engine into a stall or climbing aboard an authentic steam engine highlights their visit. Others prefer to enter the century-old Denver & Rio Grande reservations office or peruse the William H. Jackson photograph collection. And many visitors return simply to watch the rail mechanics at work and inspect this historic trainline's ever changing collections.

For information on schedules and rates, write or call the railroad at 479 Main Avenue, Durango, Colorado 81301, (970)- 247-2733.

The Cascade Canyon Train follows the Highline above the Rockwood Gorge.

THE WINTER-TO-SPRING CASCADE CANYON TRAIN

About the time winter's blanket has quieted the town, the familiar mournful whistle of the D&SNGRR calls out for a new kind of snowy adventure. It's a ride aboard the Cascade Canyon train as it travels the white-quilted majesty of the Animas Valley to a riverside stop at Cascade Canyon.

The winter train season begins on the day before Thanksgiving and continues daily through early May. Departing from the downtown depot at 10 a.m., it arrives two hours later at the Cascade Wye for a one-hour lunch stop. Located 26 miles from Durango, the broad, flat area in the canyon is large enough to accommodate a wye, the curved track used to turn the engine and up to 14 passenger cars around. A few miles beyond this point, danger begins. Even an Iron Horse won't venture into this region, one of the most avalanche-prone areas of America.

However, before the snow becomes impenetrable, on the Saturday before Christmas, Santa steps aboard the Cascade Canyon train. As he arrives at the Durango Depot, hundreds of children greet him, eager to sit on his lap and share with him their dreams of toys.

Tangled in a curling column of black and gray smoke, the train leaves the snowy Durango depot, announcing its passage through town using a prescribed selection of long and short whistles. As it reaches the Animas Valley, herds of winter-ing elk pose for passengers' cameras. The forested valley closes in, nearly touching the train windows with its snow-laden branches. The season's white and quiet preside.

Snowflakes whiten the Durango depot.

Then the smoke-and-cinder belching engine hisses to a steaming stop at the Cascade Wye. Most passengers don their boots and coats here to venture beyond the comforts of the passenger or parlor cars. Rabbit and deer tracks punctuate the snow-blanketed forest. Occasionally, elk scatter through the stands of spruce. Just 20 yards away, the Animas River beckons, crackling quietly beside its ice-laced shores. Pillows of snow cling to the river rocks. The backdrop of towering white pinnacles, the spine of the San Juan Mountains, completes this wilderness winterscape.

Some passengers prefer to snack and visit at the picnic tables stationed in this lovely setting. Others wander back to the hissing black engine for a close-up look at the steam locomotive. Its snowplow, spanning 11 feet, was newly built in D&SNGRR's roundhouse as a replica of a 1920s original. Its 6-foot height is capable of clearing 18 to 24 inches of freshly fallen snow. Railroad buffs perform hands-and-knees inspections here to examine the loco-motive's flange blades, designed to clear snow and ice accumulations along the inside of the rail. Those lingering may chance to see the fireman load coal in the fire-box that drives the train. And nearly everyone with a camera poses for a shot of themselves beside Durango's own Iron Horse steaming in its snowy pasture.

With the engineer's four blasts, passengers are called back to step aboard the Cascade Canyon train for the return trip to Durango. Basking in the warmth and familiarity of their assigned seats, they can relax and sometimes snooze. They remember snow and laughter and the season at its finest.

Pictographs at the Falls Creek Rock Shelter are believed to be of the early Basketmaker era, 400 to 600 A.D.

●

Hidden Valley, site of Falls Creek, featured abundant and diverse resources for the prehistoric populations living there.

ANCIENT PUEBLOAN BEGINNINGS

Long before 900 A.D. when ancestral Pueblo and Hopi clans began chiseling stones for their cliff houses at Mesa Verde, the Animas Valley's first inhabitants had been established for more than 1,000 years.

The Ancient Puebloans, whom archaeologists refer to as Basketmakers, occupied rock shelters and pithouses throughout the Animas Valley and its environs. Their widespread, continuous habitation of the region, from 300 B.C. to 800 A.D., is recognized as the earliest and longest of the hunter-gatherers in the Southwest.

These prehistoric people began farming in the Animas Valley, planting corn and squash in the terraces above it, kindling their transition to an agricultural society. They also hunted deer, elk and small game, living in an area archaeologist Earl Morris called, "a close approach to paradise."

Basketmaker houses at Falls Creek were single-room dwellings placed on talus slopes and rock shelter floors. The structures were 20-30 feet in diameter with a shallow depression for a floor and walls of logs laid horizontally, waterproofed with ample mud mortar. Later, Basketmaker dwellings were deep pithouses of mud and timber construction. Both housing styles reflect occupation during the Basketmaker period. Remnants of this era of Ancient Puebloan habitation have been found throughout the Animas Valley and south near Bodo Park. By the 10th century A.D., these early inhabitants migrated as clans from the area, a practice of their spiritual beliefs. In the 16th century, Ute Indians and other clans may have used these same sites.

Most notable amongst the remaining sites is the Falls Creek Rock Shelters, located six miles north of Durango in a narrow basin paralleling the Animas Valley off County Road 204.

Potsherds and corncobs are remnants of an ancient but still-thriving Southwestern culture.

Discovered in 1937 by amateur archaeologist Helen Sloan Daniels, who conveyed the information to Zeke Flora, Falls Creek's two rock terraces serve as platforms for single room dwellings. Flora opened the site's burial crevice and removed 19 skeletons, allowing a perfectly mummified body he named "Esther" to be shown publicly. At the request of the American Indian Movement, the body is now housed at the Mesa Verde laboratory.

Immediately following Flora's finding, archaeologist Earl Morris studied the site and its cultural remnants. Sections of woven human hair, doeskin wrappings, sandals, cradleboard and baskets were among the rarely seen, perishable items found there.

Morris' evaluations proved that the Basketmaker people built permanent homes and knew how to grind the corn they grew, two previously unaccepted theories.

Most of the materials from the Falls Creek site have been dispersed into separate collections, though some remain on display at the Mesa Verde Museum. The Falls Creek site is but a small region contained in what many archaeologists consider one of the earliest indications of Ancient Puebloan civilization. Today, these sites remain as important cultural, spiritual and ethnic links to the Pueblo, Hopi and Zuni people.

Due to the extreme cultural and scientific sensitivity and the highly fragile nature of the Falls Creek Rock Shelters, the Forest Service has suspended all public access to the shelters. The Forest Service is currently discussing appropriate permanent management strategies with Native Americans, the scientific community and the public.

Call the Forest Service at (970) 247-4874 for more information.

A COWBOY DISCOVERY

On a snowy December morning in 1881, two cowboys set out to track down stray cattle. They probably never found the lost "doggies." What they did find not only changed their lives but the lives of almost everyone who has ever visited or lived in Southwest Colorado.

Charlie Mason along with his companion Richard Wetherill stumbled upon America's greatest archaeological treasure at Mesa Verde. Mason said later, "We rode out to the point of the mesa … From the rim of the canyon we had our first view of Cliff Palace, just across the canyon from us. To me, this is the grandest view of all among the ancient ruins of the Southwest." So began a new era in Durango.

Several months after Mason, Wetherill and companions had taken truckloads of ancient artifacts from Mesa Verde, Durangoans had their first chance at buying what *The Durango Morning Herald* called "1,000 rare relics and valuable specimens." There were many browsers but no buyers.

Meanwhile, Benjamin Wetherill, fully aware of the significance of his son's findings, wrote to the Smithsonian Institution to ask about selling the collected relics. Strapped for funds, they too declined the proffered purchase.

As the Wetherills continued digging at Mesa Verde, their motives evolved from collecting to preserving. In his ongoing correspondence with the Smithsonian,

B. K. Wetherill described his son's activities and style. "We keep a strict record of all our discoveries, where found, etc., and all other items of interest," he noted in a December 1889 letter. Two months later, the senior Wetherill wrote with remarkable insight, "We are particular to preserve the buildings but fear, unless the Govt. sees proper to make a national park of the canyons

Rangers lead tours of Cliff Palace, the largest cliff dwelling in North America.

including Mesa Verde, the tourists will destroy them."

After the Durango showing, the Wetherills took their collection to Pueblo and later to Denver. The Colorado Historical Society became the first buyer of the Wetherill's work, and today this collection is on display in the Society's museum in Denver.

As news of the former cowboys' intriguing discoveries spread, Wetherill's Alamo Ranch in Mancos became the starting point for tours to Mesa Verde. One of the more avid tourists was Frederick Chapin. His explorations of the ruins and cañons resulted in a portfolio of fine photographs and detailed descriptions that drew national attention.

Another visitor was Swedish scholar Gustav Nordenskiold, who came to the Southwest seeking a warm, dry climate for his tuberculosis and heard of the Indian dwellings. Intending to stay one week at Mesa Verde, he instead spent months using scientific methods to collect and evaluate artifacts. His work ranks as the first conscientious endeavor to excavate and record Mesa Verde's archaeology systematically. He compiled his observations in the respected book, The Cliff Dwellers of the Mesa Verde.

However, Durangoans and all Native Americans were outraged at Nordenskiold's expedition, believing it was one of looting and spiritual desecration. Yet, complaints filed against him were dismissed since there were no laws prohibiting him from his research. A Durango women's group reacted by petitioning the U.S. government to protect Mesa Verde as a national park. Their demands were met in 1906. Today, the park incorporates Native American beliefs into interpretations heard and read by 700,000 visitors annually.

Star trails etch the night sky at Chaco Canyon's Pueblo Bonito, the largest Ancestral Puebloan dwelling in the world.

●

Luminarias glowed at Spruce Tree House during a winter celebration at Mesa Verde. In respect to all cultures and the fragile nature of these ancient sites, candle lighting and similar practices no longer occur at Mesa Verde and other archaeological sites.

WHERE THE SPIRITS DWELL

A pair of steel tracks links Durango to its railroad past, while a paved highway connects the town to one of the most artistic yet mysterious chapters in human history - Mesa Verde. Located 35 miles west of Durango, Mesa Verde National Park remains the world's first park dedicated to preserving the works of ancient people. Its most famous structures, sandstone palaces clinging to cliffsides and underground circular ceremonial rooms called kivas, represent a thin though stunning slice of the culture developed there.

Ancient Puebloans, once called Anasazi, began settling in Mesa Verde around 500 A. D. and migrated east and south around 1300. During their seven-century occupation, these primitive people without a written language or use of the wheel, metal or horse developed a lifestyle that evolved from a sustenance existence to a society of farmers, potters, weavers and stonemasons. They traded their surplus items with distant communities via a complex network of roads and trails. Pithouses clustered into villages on the mesa top or cliff terraces served as shelters for the first people of Mesa Verde, called Basketmakers by archaeologists.

This settled way of life gave way to farming corn and squash, lessening their dependency on hunting and gathering practices. The Ancient Puebloans learned to make pottery that eventually replaced their finely woven baskets. By 750 their population had swelled. Homes were above ground, made of upright poles supporting walls of

mud and branches. A few pithouses remained, perhaps as predecessors to kivas.

Stone masonry in Mesa Verde became a new skill by 1000 A.D. Groups of two- and three-story buildings housed entire villages on the mesa tops, much of which was cleared for farming.

During Mesa Verde's classic period, 1100 to 1300 A.D., the population may have

Mesa Verde's Oak Tree House in winter

reached several thousand. Many of its villages, consisting of small room clusters and large pueblos with enclosed kivas, remain standing as testimony to the builders' skill. Pueblo walls were built of carefully shaped stones laid in a straight course, yet following the contours of the area in which they were placed. Round towers

also appeared during this time. Puebloan pottery reached its highest level; its designs of black drawings on white background are still copied today.

A reversal of lifestyles occurred around 1200. After centuries of life on the mesa top, the early Puebloans moved back to the cliff alcoves, a shelter their ancestors had previously occupied. No one knows for certain why they moved. Perhaps protection from the elements or enemies was their motive. Religious or psychological reasons may have caused their move. The region's documented 25-year drought may have been the deciding factor. Yet, the grandeur of such dwellings as Cliff Palace and Balcony House transcends this unanswered question.

After a century of scientific scrutiny, ranging from the study of a tower's solar alignment to the examination of a burial site's pollen samples, new understandings are still emerging. Contemporary Pueblo people are sharing their cultural and spiritual links to Mesa Verde. Their explanations to such questions as why their ancestors left Mesa Verde and what their religious values were are now a part of the park's ever-evolving interpretive program.

As visitors to Mesa Verde ponder these interpretations, some actually hear a *mano* rhythmically grinding corn on a *matate* or smell the pungent smoke of a piñon fire. Or feel a spiritual presence while immersed in the cool darkness of a kiva. It's the "spirit of those who came before" that touches people as they walk the sandy paths at Mesa Verde.

Like the ruins of a medieval palace, Hovenweep Castle clings to the canyon rim at Hovenweep National Monument.

PATHWAYS TO A CULTURAL COMPLEX

Masters of masonry, the Ancient Puebloans (formerly called Anasazi), left their remarkable stonework strewn across the area now known as the Four Corners. From 1100 to 1300, their population may have numbered 30,000. Thousands of their dwellings, towers and kivas (underground ceremonial rooms) dot the landscape. Still, after a century of study and speculation, new understandings about these sites and their occupants are continually emerging. Durango serves as the starting point to many interpreted sites where these people slept, cooked, prayed and played.

Salmon Ruins, a pueblo south of Durango, near Bloomfield, New Mexico, represents the Chaco Canyon Culture, people highly skilled in road building and astronomy. Nearby is Aztec Ruin, where visitors take self-guided tours to the large pueblo and a great kiva.

Chimney Rock Archaeological Area is believed to be an outlier in the Chacoan Empire, isolated from other Ancient Pueblo communities. Its twin spires, seen from U.S. Highway 160, some 45 miles east of Durango, were home and sacred shrine to the early Puebloans who farmed the area. Guided tours of Chimney Rock pass numerous dwellings, kivas and unexplained stone remnants.

South of Mesa Verde within the Ute Mountain Reservation lies the 125,000-acre Ute Mountain Park. Reservations for tours are necessary for visits to this minimally developed area where hundreds of dwellings, rock images and cliff structures blend with the canyon landscape.

The Anasazi Heritage Center, located near Dolores, 45 miles northwest of Durango, features a wheelchair-accessible walk to a Ancestral Puebloan village discovered during the Dominguez-Escalante Expedition of 1776. The museum here houses over a million Ancient Puebloan artifacts collected before the nearby McPhee Reservoir dam was built.

Crow Canyon Archaeological Center, just 3.5 miles northwest of Cortez, maintains ongoing digs at several sites. Participants in the center's seminars on Ancient Pueblo life combine classroom lectures with site interpretation and excavation as well as processing artifacts in a laboratory. Day visits to other archaeological excavation sites may be arranged. For more information, call (800) 422-8975.

Lowrey Pueblo Ruins at aptly named Pleasant View, about 20 miles northwest of Cortez, features a quiet tour of an 11th and 12th century, above-ground pueblo marked by two remarkable kivas. The great kiva here, 45 feet in diameter, is one of the largest ever discovered, suggesting this pueblo may have been a religious or trading center.

Straddling the Colorado-Utah border sits Hovenweep National Monument. Several self-guided trails lead visitors past a variety of oval, square, circular and D-shaped towers. Rangers also provide directions to outlying ruins.

Perhaps the most intriguing of the Ancestral Pueblo centers is Chaco Canyon, 21 miles south of New Mexico Highway 44, 35 miles southeast of Bloomfield. Honeycombed with ruins but without a grave to be found, this ancient community once housed what archaeologists and Native Americans believe was a very sophisticated culture.

Incorporating contemporary Native American beliefs into the interpretation of these and other Ancient Pueblo sites is yet another lure that draws people to Durango and the Southwest again and again.

Ute Chief Buckskin Charlie (fourth from the right) stands with his family. With the 1890 death of Chief Ouray, Buckskin Charlie became the first Ute leader to head his people during the reservation period.
Animas Museum

U.S. Senator Ben Nighthorse Campbell, from Ignacio, Colorado dons his Cheyenne war bonnet and buckskins for Durango's annual Fiesta Days Parade. Elected in 1992, Campbell reigns as the only Native American in Congress.

SOUTHWEST COLORADO'S TRUE NATIVE PEOPLE

Nowhere is access to the Native American past and present more direct than in Durango. Ancient Pueblo settlements dot the region south of town. Edging the state's southern border sit two reservations – small, dry remnants of the Ute domain that once blanketed western Colorado and parts of Utah and New Mexico. Once a tribe of seven loosely aligned bands, Colorado's Ute Indians now consist of two tribes. The Southern Utes, a blend of Capote and Mouache bands, reside on a narrow, 75-mile long reservation near the town of Ignacio, 25 miles southeast of Durango. The Ute Mountain Utes, known as the Weenuche, claim the 475,000-acre tract near Towoac, 55 miles southwest of Durango.

Both groups share a tragic chapter in the story of Native American people. It began in 1868, when the U. S. government granted Chief Ouray and the Ute Indians all of western Colorado. Within five years, the mood of protection had changed as silver and gold strikes in the San Juan Mountains lured legions of prospectors, driven more by greed for mineral wealth than the era's manifest destiny.

Avoiding a potentially disastrous consequence, Chief Ouray signed the Brunot Agreement on September 13, 1873, relinquishing over four million acres of the San Juan Mountains to the U. S. government.

Justification for another government-imposed Ute relocation was the Meeker Massacre of 1879 in northwestern Colorado that resulted in southwestern Colorado's Southern Ute Reservation.

Not all tribes would assume the region's enforced farming lifestyle. Former

Both the Southern Utes and Ute Mountan Utes hold intertribal pow-wows open to the public.

hunters and warriors, the Weenuche fled west after 10 years to a parched, alien desert which further reduced them as a people. Eventually they set up camp on the western edge of the Southern Ute Reservation. Today they are based in Towoac, at the foot of the mountain known as the Sleeping Ute. Shaped like a woman lying on her back, her face turned west away from the mountains, she symbolizes the Weenuche's final departure from their former domain. This is but one of the many legends that describes this famous mountain profile west of Cortez. Despite a century of cultural deprivations, both tribes have revived their heritage and made steps for the future.

The 1,200-member Southern Ute tribe has conceived a two-fold economic plan based on natural resources and tourism. Oil and gas development on the reservation contributes the majority of the tribe's revenues. Tourism fosters artistic traditions including beadwork, pottery and weavings on display in the Sky Ute Gallery in Ignacio. Other attractions to the reservation include the Southern Ute Cultural Center and Museum that houses hundreds of historical and archaeological artifacts and the dance performances of the Southern Ute Heritage Performing Artists. High stakes gambling at Sky Ute Casino also contributes to the tribe's financial base.

With unemployment in Colorado often highest in Towoac, economic recovery for the 1,700 Ute Mountain Utes is often fueled by gambling at the recently built casino. Tourism at Ute Mountain Tribal Park, a 125,000-acre cultural preserve adjacent to Mesa Verde, is another mainstay. Tribal-owned and operated Ute Mountain Pottery produces hand-painted, high-gloss vessels, also contributing to the tribe's budget.

Remaining few but proud, the members of Southwest Colorado's Ute tribes are cultivating a heritage nearly devastated by white settlement, building upon their innate talents and the area's natural resources.

On July 6, 1998, boulders bus-sized and smaller broke from the Dakota sandstone rim of the Animas Valley's Missionary Ridge, scouring a swath 200 feet wide and 600 feet long. Rockslides of this kind and magnitude occur perhaps every thousand years.

Geologic Formations of Animas Valley

- Dakota Sandstone
- Morrison Formation
- Junction Creek SS
- Wanaka Formation
- Entrada Sandstone
- Navajo Sandstone
- Cutler Formation
- Hermosa Formation

Glacial Moraine

OF MOUNTAINS, MORAINES AND MEADOWS

Beckoning yet barricading, the San Juan Mountains' sky-piercing crags and forest-clad slopes have long been a source of sustenance, wealth and inspiration for many who have ventured near them. Legends flourish from deep in their crevices, where hunters aim, miners pick and geologists examine. One of the newest, most studied stories tells of the mountain-building history of the Colorado Rockies' southernmost range.

Skimming the chapter on Continental Drift, mountain-building began around two billion years ago. Pressures within the earth's crust moved to the North American plate and pushed a weak zone skyward, now known as the Rocky Mountains. Clues to the San Juan's Precambrian beginning can be found in the pink granite of the Needle Mountains, the quartzite near Elk Park and the metamorphic gneiss of the West Needles.

Erosion nearly flattened the mountain upstart at least three times during the Precambrian chapter until the Paleozoic seas contributed their sediments, adding meat to the mountain's backbones.

Rumblings within the Colorado landscape began around 300 million years ago when two ancestral mountain ranges were lifted from the seas. After repeated periods of flooding and silting, the Front Range

formed where the eastern most of the pair stood. The western partner, the Uncompahgria, left a fraction of its legacy of erosion in the red-rock Hermosa cliffs that rise 2,000 feet above the Animas Valley.

Renewed rumblings worldwide brought about the next rather fiery chapter. Known as the Laramide Orogeny, great

Cutler and Hermosa sandstone forms the red cliffs flanking the eastern side of the glacier-carved Animas Valley.

mountain ranges, including the Rockies, rose up in the form of faulted anticlines 65 million years ago. The San Juans, however, were forming at this time from a huge dome a hundred miles broad. As erosion exposed the dome's Precambrian rock, volcanoes began spewing dust, rocks and lava, burying the landscape a mile deep in

places. The most recent burst of volcanic activity, 25 million years ago, blanketed the San Juans in black basalt, evidenced in the dark gray rock seen in the road cuts near South Fork, Colorado. The gigantic volcanoes caved in, leaving collapsed volcanic calderas such as those seen as the ring of mountains surrounding Silverton.

Erosive sculpture marks the final, ongoing chapter in the San Juans, continuing in the form of wind, water and frost. Perhaps the most dramatic and visible agent of erosion is glaciers. Though Colorado was not in the path of the four major periods of continental glaciation, icecaps covered most of the San Juans beginning about 2 million years ago. Some 10,000 years ago, the largest of these icecaps, called the Animas Glacier, extended as far south as Animas City (north Durango). It carved pinnacles into the Needle Mountains, scooped out alpine lakes like Little and Big Molas and shaped the Animas Valley, leaving in its path rocky deposits called moraines.

Shallow glacial lakes formed along these moraines and later filled with soil, forming meadows where elk graze today. The Animas River lazily ox-bows through here, resting so it appears after its tumultuous passage from the upper Animas Valley's narrow, constrained walls.

Built in 1902, the second Trimble Hot Springs hotel called the Hermosa House reflects a highpoint in popularity and elegance in Trimble history. Photo courtesy Trimble Hot Springs

Water heated far beneath the La Plata Mountains surfaces at Trimble Hot Springs. An Olympic-sized pool, soaking tubs, snack bar and massage room are among the amenities guests enjoy here.

FORTUNES IN ROCK AND WATER

A new chapter in San Juan history began one fateful day in 1860 when explorer Charles Baker found flecks of gold sparkling in a stream above what is now known as Silverton. Thirteen years later, an estimated 4,000 treasure hunters spread across the region's slopes, tunneling mines and establishing communities – all dependent on the newly laid Denver and Rio Grande Railroad line. Durango, the train's southern headquarters, became the springboard for the San Juan gold then silver stampede.

The mining era was a brief though furious period leaving hundreds of faded wooden remnants dotting the high country above Durango. The nearest of these ghost towns is actually one of the first settlements in south-western Colorado – Animas City No. 1.

The winter following his discovery, Baker and his crew, fleeing Indian conflicts and lack of supplies, struggled down the Animas Valley and established camp near what is now called Baker's Bridge. The call of the Civil War and the little luck in finding gold ore forced Baker and the settlement's 300 frustrated miners to move on. Their settlement, which later became Animas City, remained nearly deserted until the Brunot Agreement of 1873 that forfeited Ute rights to the San Juan Mountains.

Nowadays, the scenic ride to Baker's Bridge follows the level, paved East Animas Road (County Road 250) 11.7 miles leading to the one-lane bridge over Baker's Chasm. Movie goers will recognize it as the famous cliff-jumping scene from the 1969 film "Butch Cassidy and the Sundance Kid."

Another memorable day trip featuring Durango's mining past and a grand vista

Mining may be a mere sentence in the geologic story of the San Juans, but the wealth it tapped triggered volumes.

begins on La Plata Canyon Road, 12 miles west of town off U. S. Highway 160. Just before the pavement ends is May Day, formerly a prosperous gold placer camp and mining town of 500 to 1,000 people. In 1876, it was the county seat, but only a few original foundations stubble the ranchland now. On the road's west side sit a group of privately-owned white frame buildings

with red trim, one of which is the May Day Schoolhouse.

A high-clearance vehicle is helpful for the 4-mile drive to La Plata City. This is considered the site where Spanish explorer Juan Maria de Rivera discovered gold when he led a party through here in 1775. A hundred years later, Yankee fortune hunters hit paydirt, mining silver along with gold until the 1893 Silver Panic all but closed the town. Proceed to the top of Kennebec Pass (four-wheel drive only) for views of the 12,000-foot high La Plata Mountains.

Regardless of the intrigue old mining shafts and their surrounding cabins have, their rotting timbers and deadly fumes pose serious threats. The majority of them are privately owned so entering them constitutes trespass, too.

An appropriate way to top a mine-visiting day is to unwind the way miners did – soaking at Trimble Hot Springs. Proclaimed in 1883 as "The Favorite Health and Pleasure Resort of the San Juans," its soothing, healing waters still flow despite three fires that devastated the resort. Guests here now enjoy an Olympic-size pool alongside several hot pools in a quiet garden setting. Trimble is located 6 miles north of Durango, west of U. S. Highway 550 at Trimble Lane.

Rising 6,000 feet above the Animas River Canyon, several life zones blanket the West Needle Mountains, part of the San Juan Mountains, the largest range in the U.S. Rockies.

●

Day hikers in the Little Molas Lake area point out the surrounding peaks. Engineer Mountain (12,968 feet) looms in the background.

A MASTERPIECE OF HABITATS

The warp and weft of a mountain masterpiece edges Durango. Towering nearly 8,000 feet above the town where weather reaches the extremes, the San Juan Mountains harbor an intricate interweaving of plants, animals, soils and climates.

A single thread of this weaving may begin in a dark tangle of oak brush. Silver-green sagebrush and daggers of yucca stubble the sunny hillside. Nearby, mule deer and rabbit find cover in a pygmy forest of piñon pine and juniper – a source of food, fuel and tools for the Ute Indians. This is considered a Foothills zone, the second of Colorado's five major life zones – the Plains (3,350-5,500 feet), Foothills (5,500-8,000 feet), Montane (8,000-9,500 feet), Sub-Alpine (9,500-11,500 feet) and Alpine (11,500-14,433 feet).

Next, the thread enters a cathedral of Ponderosa pines fanning their branches of long needles 50 feet above the forest floor. Flickering patterns of sunlight and patches of cinnamon-red bark paint a stained glass mosaic in the thinly vegetated undercover. Amidst the music of wind in the pines, chickadees chirp and Stellar jays screech. Pine squirrels send long scoldings. Stands of the shorter-needled spruce and fir trees root in neighboring north-facing regions. This is a transitional zone, delightfully experienced along Hermosa Creek Trail, 10 miles north of town.

Moving into the next, cooler, wetter region, the Montane zone, aspens make their debut. Splashing gold across the slopes each fall, they appear to announce their triumph as forest healers. Almost immediately after a fire, aspens sprout from a long-established root system, growing to maturity in 25 to 50 years. Their fallen leaves accumulate over time into a deep loam that serves as bedding for saplings destined to replace them – Douglas fir and Ponderosa pine. Trademark rubbings of

The Columbine, Colorado's state flower, thrives in moist, cool habitats of the Sub-Alpine zone.

deer and elk or territorial scratches of bear mark many aspens here. The trail to Potato Lake, about 30 miles north of Durango, winds through a Montane forest.

Wildflowers speckle pinks, yellows and lavenders throughout the Sub-Alpine zone where thick forests of spruce and fir border open meadows. Blue columbine, protected as Colorado's state flower, thrive in a variety of moist, cool habitats of the San Juan uplands. Mountain goats transplanted into the San Juan's Needle Range in 1971 by the Colorado Division of Wildlife roam the upper reaches of this zone. Wind, an ever-present force here, shapes the upper-most edge of tree stands, chiseling them with 100-mile-an-hour forces into contorted forms known as *krummholz*. A popular climb to Engineer Peak (12,968 feet), starting at the summit of Coal Bank Pass, meanders through Sub-Alpine regions then tops off with spectacular views into the Alpine zone.

Diminutive wildflowers dot this zone's top-of-the-world landscape dominated by drying winds and a brief growing season. Picas and marmots frequently scamper its lichen-quilted boulders, broadcasting piercing chirps. On rare occasions, the Uncompahgre fritillary, a small, inconspicuous butterfly recently added to the endangered species list, is sighted in the San Juans fluttering above snowfields. This is indeed the most fragile of life zones.

Woven throughout the mountain tapestry are the silvery threads of riparian zones. Formed along streams, rivers, lakes and ponds, these wet habitats foster lush growth. As much as 80 percent of Colorado wildlife depends on riparian zones for water, food and cover. One such creature, the magnificent bald eagle, also an endangered species, commonly forages the open waters of the Animas River during its winter migration.

Sunrise paints the morning clouds above the Sneffles Range, north of Durango.

●

Early Durangoans set out on an overnight trek in the San Juan Mountains, circa 1900.

Grand Landscapes to Encounter

Interwoven layers of natural splendor blanket the San Juans, the single largest range in the Rocky Mountains. Little wonder a growing number of people from across the nation and abroad take their first steps into the 1.9 million-acre expanse at nearby trailheads.

Beginning within Durango's city limits, a number of trails features a peak ascent and is often accessible year-round. Animas City Mountain, Twin Buttes and Perin's Peak are popular destinations to hike that rate from easy to challenging.

Those wanting to explore the southern section of the Colorado Trail, the 469-mile alpine path between Denver and Durango, access it 3.5 miles west of Main Avenue on the Junction Creek Road (25th St.). Eight miles beyond the Colorado Trailhead, on the graveled Forest Road #543, the 0.6-mile Animas Overlook Trail begins. This state-of-the-art wheelchair accessible, interpreted trail features signposts and viewpoints that describe the diverse forces that shaped this corner of the state.

A maze of dirt roads and footpaths serve as trails to the old mining camps and alpine meadows of the La Plata Mountains, accessed just 12-miles west of town on the La Plata Canyon Road (County Road 124). Hikers share the trails with mountain bikers, so caution is advised.

Untold pathways into the San Juan National Forest's valleys and peaks begin along the highway corridor heading north of Durango on U. S. 550.

The Goulding Creek Trail provides a moderately challenging 6-mile hike through aspen groves and meadows of lupine before entering Hermosa Cliffs, 17 miles north of Durango near Tamarron Resort.

Aspens canopy hikers during much of their 4-mile, 1,100-feet plunge to the Animas River via the Purgatory Trail,

Flowering lupine highlights early summer hikes in the alpine meadows of the San Juan Mountains.

located a half-mile south of the ski area on the opposite side of the road. The flat areas on both sides of the river serve as relaxing destinations before heading up again.

Backpackers continue hiking north 5.5 miles on the river's east side before reaching the Columbine Pass Trail, a prime artery into the Weminuche Wilderness, the heart of the San Juans.

Named for the band of Ute Indians that once inhabited the area, the 405,031-acre Weminuche area is the state's largest wilderness. When expedition leader John Charles Fremont first eyed this morass of peaks in the winter of 1849, he called it "one of the highest, most rugged and impractical of all of the Rocky Mountain Ranges, inaccessible to the trappers and hunters even in the summer's time."

Backpackers now access it via several nearby trails. The most novel way begins on the Durango and Silverton Narrow Gauge Railroad. Daily scheduled stops at Elk Park and Needleton bring hikers to starting points in the region's 500-mile trail network. However, a wilderness experience here is often shared; ease of access allowed by the train coupled with the area's proximity to three of the state's prestigious "fourteeners" (peaks over 14,000 feet in height) have made these the Weminuche's most-peopled destinations. "No-trace" camping practices are essential here.

For a select few, however, walking all or sections of the 80-mile Continental Divide Trail contained in the Weminuche is the ultimate outdoor experience.

For further information regarding trails in the area, contact the Visitor Information Service for the U. S. Forest Service in Durango at (970) 247-4874.

Posed in the path of Pacific storms, the San Juan Mountains receive some of the highest snowfalls in the West and decidedly the most avalanches.

SAFE CLEARINGS

As expected, winter's claws take hold with an annual post-Thanksgiving snowstorm. Its grip deepens as snowfalls reach average totals of 400 inches at Wolf Creek, 300 inches at Purgatory and 70 inches in Durango. Mobility on the Southwest's highways is critical and precarious.

With each snowfall, tranquility settles in temporarily. Highway 550 becomes a white swath bisecting snowy slopes. Spruce trees stand alongside it, immobile, burdened under the latest storm's blanket. Above, a red-tailed hawk circles the turquoise sky, surveying its silent, still domain. Watchful for winged predators, a snowshoe hare tentatively hops to a clearing. Suddenly, in leaps of nearly 9 feet, it dashes for the brush. The hawk swoops down, its talons miss the prey, its wings kiss the snow.

Then a snowplow's scraping, rumbling roar, muffled by 12 inches of powder, invades the alpine realm of Coal Bank Pass, altitude 10,640 feet. A pick-up truck with chains gripping its tires, rattles onward, undeterred. A stream of four-wheel-drive wagons and two-wheel-drive sedans follows behind a sander-plow truck.

Invariably, Colorado's Lead Avalanche Forecasters will be driving one of the first vehicles on the newly cleared road. They will stop repeatedly to analyze snowpack on the 40-mile stretch north of Durango, considered the most avalanche-prone section of highway in North America.

The avalanche pros look for accumulations of an inch or more an hour and check for rapid temperature change and wind shift. They note snowflake shape on slopes of 30 to 45 degrees; icy needle or pellet-like shapes create less stable conditions than the classic star-shape snowflakes.

Snow clearing and removal receives top priority in Durango where crews sometimes work 24 hours a day.

Given the natural order of mountain winters, an avalanche could bury this roadway for the winter and spring. However, these winter warriors oversee 206 avalanche paths, releasing deadly build-ups that could entomb snowplows and passenger cars.

Using Avalaunchers, gas cannons attached to the top of a truck, they launch explosives that shake loose many small slides. Another tool, the Howitzer cannon, used in the Korean War, allows accurate targeting on avalanche starting zones located a distance from the highway. To release snow in remote avalanche paths, crews aboard helicopters drop explosives.

The March 1992 avalanche that claimed the life of a snowplow driver working just 200 feet outside a snowshed above Ouray triggered the hiring of avalanche experts. Their skills were immediately put to work. Record snow amounts dominated the winter of 1992-93, and yet their vigilance at releasing mini-avalanches kept Red Mountain Pass open with the exception of four occasions lasting longer than 12 hours.

That same season, in the valley below, Durango's snow removal crews cleared an amount nearly twice the average by hauling 129 inches of snow – 24 hours a day, for 5 weeks.

In an era when heroes are television cowboys dressed in white, today's western trail blazers are most certainly the ones in white.

Snowboarding has become one of the most popular winter sports around Durango.

With four ski areas located in the West's snowiest range, the San Juan Mountains offer some of the most magnificent powder in the Rockies.

A SOUTHWESTERN SKI BONANZA

The winter months bless Durango with a balance of snow and sunshine, creating a variety of edens few skiers can resist.

Among the most popular of the powdery destinations nestled in the San Juan Mountains is the Purgatory Ski Area. Located 25 miles north, the 675-acre resort is now distinguished as the Southwest's best family-oriented ski center.

Expanding winter recreation for everyone with physical or mental disabilities is the Adaptive Sports Association, based at the Purgatory Ski Area. Specialized instruction provided by the group's trained volunteers has increased self-esteem and physical well-being for hundreds of participants each year. One of ASA's more heartwarming events occurs mid-winter when two dozen National Football League Players trade their helmets for skis to join disabled skiers in parties, clinics and friendly competition.

Nearby Hesperus Ski Area, just 12 miles west of town, caters to families and groups. Affordable lift tickets and all levels of friendly terrain add to its appeal. Snowboarders flock to Hesperus' special boarding area.

The San Juan's snowy splendor is also shared by Telluride Ski Resort, 118 miles northwest of Durango. "Steep and Deep" clinics held here attest to the area's challenging reputation. Intermediate slopes abound on the mountain's west side near the ski village.

Powder hounds head to Wolf Creek Ski Area, 80 miles east of Durango. Standing here atop the Continental Divide, where snowfalls average 400 to 500 inches annually, tops most anyone's winter experience.

Skiers looking for more intimate and less expensive ski trips explore the Southwest's slopes using cross country gear ranging from flexible touring shoes and lightweight skis to rigid telemark boots and metal-edged skis. In town, both skate and track skiers tour five miles or more of looped and groomed trails at Hillcrest Golf Club, adjacent to Fort Lewis College.

Thirty-two miles of trails groomed for track and skate skiing are but one feature of Chicken Creek Ski Area, 34 miles west, near Mancos. The main section offers 20 miles of a double-tracked trail for companion skiing and a lane for skate skiers. Snowmobiles and dogs are prohibited from the trails. Better yet, skiing at this community and Forest Service-operated model project site is free!

Vallecito Lake, nestled in a mountain basin 15 miles northeast of Durango, hosts

Volunteer Adaptive Sports Association instructor coaches disabled skier in a sit ski during a full-day private lesson.

the area's newest track and skate ski system. Six miles of groomed trails here follow gentle terrain affording views of 14,000-foot peaks within the Weminuche Wilderness. Portions of this trail system edge the lake, Colorado's second largest reservoir. Supported by skier donations and managed by the Pine Valley Ski Club, the trail begins on the lake's east side.

Haviland Lake, 17 miles north of Durango, provides novice cross-country skiers the level terrain of an unplowed campground nestled in a Ponderosa pine forest. Near here, three miles of an old wagon road completes a roller-coaster loop trail marked with XC (cross-country) signs.

Purgatory's Nordic Center, located opposite the ski area's main entrance, contains 9.6 miles (16 kilometers) of groomed trails that capitalize on stunning views of the San Juans, particularly the West Needles. Classic and skate ski lessons are offered; a small trail fee is charged.

The San Juan Mountains present limitless options for unparalleled ski ventures. To the north, the gently rolling alpine slopes of Andrews Lake near Molas Pass (10,910 feet) are an ideal introduction to mountain winter touring. Beyond the lake, backcountry ski enthusiasts climb to windswept crests where their trail of powdery telemark turns begins.

Snowshoeing, one of the winter's fastest growing activities, allows nearly anyone to enjoy Durango's backyard to backcountry terrain. Snowshoe rentals and suggestions for areas to explore are available at several local sporting good stores.

Backcountry snow adventures can be dangerous. Avalanches, hypothermia, frostbite and getting lost are just some of the hazards present. Be prepared with adequate equipment, sufficient food and water, additional clothing and a reliable map. Never ski alone. Before heading out, let someone know where your party is going and when you expect to be back. Call the Avalanche Hotline at (970) 247-8187 for current information on snow conditions.

Hot air ballons float above Durango during the mid-winter carnival called Snowdown.

Broomball players, wielding straw sticks, slip, slide and occasionally score in this annual Snowdown competition.

A Wacky Winter Diversion

Along about mid-winter, skier and non-skiers alike begin asking themselves, "When was the last time I really had fun?"

That's a sure sign of cabin fever. In Durango, the cure for this malady is Snowdown, five days of zany events destined to bring out the fun-loving kid in everyone.

In line with a kid's allowance, most of the 60 or more scheduled events are free, and the ones that do charge return the fees as prize money.

Conceived in 1978 as a diversion for a long, small-town winter, Snowdown has become one of the largest, most creative outlets of winter fun anywhere. And because hundreds of volunteers dream up and organize the homespun fun, community involvement is contagious.

Most of the events take place in the heart of Durango: behind swinging bar doors, atop ice skating rinks and hills-turned-ski-slopes, around the fairground's snow-packed race ring and in restaurant parking lots scattered throughout town.

Months before the first snowflakes fall, a contest for the Snowdown theme shapes the character of each year's carnival. One such winner, "What goes up must Snowdown," got played up (and down) during the events, and the yo-yo was selected as the year's Snowdown theme toy.

Other toys such as hotel beds, toilet seats, brooms and tricycles appear in such veteran events as the Snowdown Bed Race, Broomball (plenty of padding and straw needed for this skate-less event held on ice) and the Waiter-Waitress Tricycle Races.

The Snowdown Jokedown usually

Spiderman soars in the Gelande Jump during Snowdown. Destined to cure cabin fever, the annual mid-winter carnival consists of 60 or more wacky events.

opens the annual cabin fever cure followed by such regulars or slightly irregulars as the Baby Crawling Contest, the Beer-Belly Contest, the Mutt & Master Gymkhana and the Fantasy Filler Ice-Cream Eating Contest.

Purr-fect for a laugh is the Feline Fashion Show, which is followed by dogs of obscure ancestry dressed in their master's notion of finery strutting across the same stage for the winning paw in the Canine Fashion Show.

A tad of talent and a flair for fun are prerequisites for the cast of Snowdown's most popular event, the Snowdown Follies. This hilarious variety show for adults only is made up of new-to-the-stage local comedians and performers. It draws hundreds of followers – many of whom wait in line outside, in winter weather, for hours just to buy their four-ticket limit.

Chapman Hill, Durango's 38-acre public ski area, has become a multiple recreation attraction and a Snowdown center. Youngsters in inner-tubes and daredevils on skis slide down the same slopes that bikers wield their wheels on in the summer months. Chapman Hill Rink, an open-air, roofed structure, hosts ice hockey and broomball in the winter months, with weddings and rollerblade hockey held there during the warmer months.

Snowdown Gelande jumping events and snowboard contests held during the festival draw almost as many fans as the hill's warm-weather mountain bike competitions. During Snowdown's annual evening hot air balloon display, skiers form a torchlight parade and fireworks sparkle in the sky. Chapman Hill literally glows.

Helmeted paddlers shoot through "No Name," one of many treacherous rapids on the Upper Animas. Considered a novelty until the late 70s, rafting has become a major industry in Durango, home base to dozens of outfitters.

A Wellspring of Vitality

Historically, the water that mountains capture, store and deliver downstream has been the lifeblood for much of humanity. So it was and is in Durango.

These days, kayaks on cartops, raft frames on pick-ups and canoes strapped to vans are a common sight in Durango. They're headed for another world, where sculpted canyons edge boulder-choked riverways. Where serene waters drift past ancient rock art. Where foaming waves thrash polished sandstone. It's the serene and spectacular river world of the Four Corners area.

The region, threaded by such white water ribbons as the Animas, San Juan, Chama, Piedra, Dolores and the mighty Colorado has become a water sports mecca. Rafting the Animas is now a top priority for most summer visitors, and rare is the resident without a river trip to boast about.

The headwaters to the area's river enthusiasm can be traced to Durango's Animas River, where national and international competitions are held, and thousands paddle its waters in kayaks, canoes and rafts each summer.

Holding the singular distinction as the only free-flowing, navigable river on the Colorado Plateau (and there are 24 main

waterways there), the Animas River remains a natural playground for water enthusiasts of every type. In 1993, Paddler Magazine named Durango "one of the top ten paddling towns in North America."

Upper Animas – to locals the very name implies expert, daring, isolated, exquisite. This 28-mile river stretch,

Morning light paints a golden backdrop for early risers on an overnight canoe trip on the Colorado River. Boating season begins in mid-April and lasts through the fall, though many professionals and fanatics train year-round at the Animas Whitewater Park.

beginning in Silverton and ending near Rockwood, drops 85 to 150 feet per mile. The few raft companies offering trips on this Class V river require their passengers to take swimming tests in the river prior to the start. Class VI is considered unrun-

nable. The thrills and rugged beauty of this wet, alpine adventure are unforgettable.

After its turbulent exit from the high country, the river flows tranquilly, following an ox-bow course in the Animas Valley. Those new to river running learn paddling techniques along this 10-mile stretch beginning about 8 miles north of Durango.

Remember to respect the rights of private property owners along this section, and watch for river hazards such as fences and trees.

The Animas "downtown" section, beginning near 32nd Street, attracts intermediate paddlers. Peppy class II water interspersed with slower stretches creates an ideal waterway for learning and fun. Whitewater Park, just south of town, is a race course for both whitewater canoeists and kayakers, with Smelter Rapid, the river's biggest (a low class III), met midway. Thousands of visitors raft this section each summer. South of the city limits, permits are required to enter the Southern Ute Indian reservation.

Given the many attributes of the Animas River and the responsible way the community uses it, it's not surprising that the Animas-La Plata Project, a proposed water diversion plan affecting Durango's river, remains a hotly debated issue.

A kayaker paddles the slalom course at Whitewater Park, located at the Visitor Center, south of downtown Durango. This premier water playground was built as a cooperative project by local businesses, Durango Parks and Recreation and hundreds of community members.

●

An "end-o" in Smelter Rapid requires strategic moves by a kayaker in Animas River Days.

WET-N-WILD WINNERS

Only three cities in the U. S. can boast of a wild, whitewater river flowing freely through them. Durango is one of the trio and uses this unique attribute most effectively and responsibly.

Each summer, despite its legendary "River of Lost Souls" name, thousands of boaters converge on the Animas for clinics, competitions or simply to watch a winning paddler maneuver his or her boat through a specifically designed course. Historically, the Animas was named the *Rio de las Animas Perdidas*, Spanish for the River of Lost Souls.

It began in 1982 as a weekend of river contests for locals. Quickly, Animas River Days grew to become Colorado's premier whitewater festival. The slalom course marked for this event instigated the Animas River's Whitewater Park, one of the few full-length, world-class slalom courses in the nation. Located near downtown Durango, the Park has rocks strategically positioned in the waterway creating a popular training ground for local paddlers and national racers.

The forces behind the development of Durango's Whitewater Park were not nature's. Rather, a true lover of rivers and one quite skilled at plying their waters – local kayaker Nancy Wiley – rallied the support of hundreds of volunteers, the Durango Area Chamber Resort Association, Durango Parks and Recreation and local business people. Their donated time

Kayaker surfs Santa Rita Hole near Whitewater Park.

and materials resulted in a state-of-the-art recreational whitewater site. Today it features permanent installations for slalom gates and underground electricity for a public address system and timing devices.

Little wonder Durango's Whitewater Park was selected in 1991 as the opening site for the prestigious Champion International Whitewater Series. Each year top kayak and canoe slalom racers from around the world compete and train here, one of the U. S. team's seven official training centers. To make the event run smoothly, hundreds of locals, paddlers and non-paddlers alike, volunteer under Wiley's direction to oversee the competitions. Similar volunteer support is used annually when the Junior Olympic Festival Qualifier is held at Whitewater Park.

Clinics held during these national events and those provided by Wiley's Four Corners Paddling School teach several hundred beginning to expert paddlers the techniques required to meet more challenging rivers. River safety and respect for the environs is a key message of every lesson. In this wet, fun way Durango's contribution to furthering environmental awareness has lasting effects.

River fun is so contagious that "raft the Animas" joins "ride the train" and "see Mesa Verde" on the must-do list of Durango's spring and summer visitors.

Fly-fishing opportunities abound in the area's mountain lakes and streams.

ANGLING FOR SERENITY

Anglers from throughout Colorado and the West are another source of river fervor in Durango. They're hooked on the variety of fishing experiences within two hours of town. The area's high mountain lakes and streams, big reservoirs and excellent rivers offer a varying kind of catch.

Durango's Animas River hosts a "Gold Medal" trout hatchery designated by the Division of Wildlife in 1997. Large rainbow and brown trout are caught in this 4-mile section south of the U.S. Highways 550 – 160 intersection. Fly and lure regulations and a two-fish, 16-inch minimum apply here. The Southern Ute Wildlife department recognizes the value of this status by enforcing the same regulations on the 2-mile section south of here. Fishing these tribally managed waters requires a special permit, available locally. In addition to fly and lure fishing, bait fishing is allowed on the Animas through downtown Durango, where Colorado's state record brown trout was caught. Some anglers ride the D&SNGRR train to Needleton or Elk Park to fish the Animas and its tributaries before heading back on a return train.

Beyond its bounty to boaters and appeal to anglers, the Animas River's future rests on the outcome of the Animas-La Plata Project. The decisions made regarding this water diversion plan first initiated in 1968 reflect how the precarious relationship between water and humans will continue in the West.

Catch and release fishing on the San Juan River's quality waters below Navajo Dam, just one hour south of Durango in New Mexico, regularly yields 14- to 16-inch trout. Bait fishing for catfish and trout is good farther below the quality area. Navajo Reservoir is a reliable source of pike, large-mouth and smallmouth bass, catfish and kokanee salmon.

Youngsters enjoy a quiet afternoon of fishing the Animas River around the turn of the century.

Backpackers bring flies and lures along for their 3-mile hike to the Weminuche Wilderness, where they fish the Pine River for brook, brown, cutthroat and rainbow trout. The trail starts near Vallecito Reservoir, 23 miles northeast of Durango. The snow-capped peaks surrounding Vallecito Reservoir provide a spectacular setting for lake fishing. Northern pike, including the former state record, and brown trout have been caught here. The lake is also known for its kokanee salmon in the fall. Several boat ramps are located along its 22-mile shoreline.

The 12-mile stretch of the Dolores River below McPhee Dam, 10 miles northwest of the town of Dolores, offers good size brown trout in a stunning pine setting. Another river fished for its beauty is the Piedra, located one hour east of Durango. Regulations specify flies and lures on the Piedra and catch and release on the Dolores.

Anglers can help reduce the spread of whirling disease, the infectious disease of trout and salmon, by disposing of fish heads or entrails in solid waste, never at the river or down the kitchen drain. And because whirling disease may spread by mud or aquatic plants, it is vital to clean boots, boats, trailers and fishing gear before leaving the access site.

Western slope bag limits for trout and salmon, except kokanee, allow two fish from streams and rivers and four fish from lakes, reservoirs and ponds.

Surrounded by so many fishing options, many of which are accessible year around, it only follows that Durango has become an angler's dream destination.

Herds of Animas Valley's winter elk rove the 3,000-acre prime habitat from late November to mid-May. Housing development in the valley has increased the pressure on land managers, residents and elected officials to develop a comprehensive plan that respects wildlife and human rights.

●

Broadcasting a deep bellow that rises in a piercing squeal, a bull elk bugles, calling his harem of cows for mating. Rutting season begins in late August and lasts through October.

MOUNTAIN MONARCHS REIGN IN ANIMAS VALLEY

Contentedly, they graze the Animas Valley's meadows, oblivious to the rush of traffic on U. S. 550. Invariably a car stops, its passengers step out and stare, astonished at the sight of 500 or more of the West's most magnificent creatures – elk.

Their presence here is both common and controversial. Historically, elk were forest and plains animals. Like bison, they traveled in herds, grazing on wild grasses. With European settlement, their destiny paralleled the bisons', and their numbers dropped down to a few hundred by 1900.

At the time, numerous Elk's Lodges had been paying top dollar for elks' teeth for use by their members. Ironically, Durango's Elk Lodge helped reverse the course on elk decline by joining the U. S. Forest Service in efforts to transplant a herd of 25 from Jackson Hole, Wyoming, to a forested area in Hermosa. The ban on elk hunting in the area from 1913 until 1931 enabled the herd size to increase. Today, the Animas Valley and a 5-mile radius surrounding it serve as a critical winter range for an estimated 2,500 to 3,000 elk.

Wapiti, a Shawnee word meaning "white rump," one of the elk's most prominent features, roam forested habitats of mountains throughout the year. In August, aspen trunks serve as posts for bull elk to rub velvet, the blood-gorged skin, from their antlers that may measure nearly 5 feet across and weigh up to 30 pounds. Discarded yearly, few racks remain in the woods as rodents quickly gnaw them for their calcium.

By mid-September, the eerie, haunting bugle of mating bulls rips the silence of the

Durango's Animas River is an important winter habitat for bald eagles. Photo © Robert Winslow, 1998

frosted hillsides. Spectacular battles occasionally break out as the 700-pound males gather and defend their harem of cows. Expending so much energy at this time causes some bulls to begin winter in poorer conditions than the cows, a fact that explains their higher winter mortality.

With the season's first heavy snows, elk descend on the Animas Valley. Throughout the winter they rove its easy terrain and fertilized alfalfa fields in herds. Elk, like people, congregate in river corridors.

As the Durango area population increases, so does the pressure on its winter elk herds, which are also growing in size. In the past decade, the Animas Valley has been partitioned by more than 70 subdivisions. Accompanying fences, pets and increased traffic cause further stress on the winter's wildlife residents.

Homeowners contend with costly fence repair and landscape destruction, while all drivers in the area face the threat of hitting an elk. Vehicle damage caused by elk collision averages $2,500 to $5,000 with mid-size vehicles and smaller cars damaged beyond repair.

A balance between wildlife needs and human rights is now being sought in Durango. Land use issues, wildlife management strategies, resident input and the inherent economic and aesthetic value of elk – these factors have brought together a broad array of land managers, developers, ranchers, elected officials and community members. No single answer exists.

Meanwhile, the health of the Animas Valley's winter elk serves as a barometer of the understanding and balance with nature Durango residents are working to achieve.

Changes in temperature and daylight allow aspen leaves to show-off their yellows and reds, colors camouflaged by chlorophyll, the tree's green food producer.

A Season's Seductions

Autumn is a temptress. She cloaks nearby mountains in shimmering golds and polishes the sky like a turquoise jewel. Art fairs abound as her kaleidoscope climaxes. Foot trails and roadways become sensory pathways of the highest pleasure.

Seductions aside, September and October in Durango are superlative. There are several ways to immerse yourself in the season's fleeting grandeur.

"Colorfest" captures the cultural and recreational best of southwestern Colorado's autumn. Durango and all the neighboring communities including Silverton, Ouray, Telluride, Cortez, Mancos, Vallecito and Ignacio celebrate this yearly festival of 70 or more events.

Hot-air balloon rallies, gallery walks, photography tours, film festivals, canoe races and runners' marathons are among the featured events in Durango during autumn. Underscoring the town's cultural heritage is the annual Durango Cowboy Gathering in which local and nationally known cowfolks share their poems and high ridin' antics.

Colorfest events happening in nearby towns are equally alluring as is the road leading to them – the San Juan Skyway. This 236-mile roadway weaves around and through southwestern Colorado's five million acres of national forest (San Juan and

Uncompahgre) and a dozen of its boom'-n'-bust or recovering towns.

Drivers adept at rubber-necking often complete the loop tour in one day. Those savoring each forest-clad mile generally spend a night or two camping or staying in hotels along the way.

To follow the official Skyway from Durango, head north 83 miles on U. S. Highway 550 to Ridgway. Aspen-gold

Travelers enjoy peak autumn colors on one of the many small roads adjoining the San Juan Skyway.

slopes compete for your attention as the highway climbs over three mountain passes, Coal Bank, Molas and Red Mountain. Stops in the towns of Silverton and Ouray along this portion are well worth the time. At the intersection of U. S. Highway 550 and State Highway 62, turn west (left) and proceed 25 miles, climbing the gentle pastures to Dallas Divide and descending to State Highway 145. Turn south (left) and continue 13 miles to the 4-mile spur road to Telluride, a gem of a town few visitors eagerly leave. Return to Highway 145 and head south (left), stopping for a good look at the remnants of the rollicking mining town of Rico and perhaps a refreshment in the riverside community of Dolores.

Cortez is found 10 miles west where U. S. Highway 160 intersects Highway 145. Take the return leg to Durango via U. S. Highway 160, pausing perhaps in the town of Mancos midway.

Many books are dedicated to the San Juan Skyway's regional attributes – its rainbow of wildflowers, its colorful and cantankerous mining or railroading history, its fantastic geological story and its amazing archaeology. Regardless, the beauty found along this drive cannot be exaggerated.

Remnants of autumn's kaleidoscope, aspen leaves lace a lake's surface. Falling leaves enliven many autumn hikes, later returning essential nutrients to the soil.

ASPEN IMMERSION

Fall color walks are like quiet, backstage visits with the season's most brilliant stars. Aspens dressed in their yellow-gold costumes rustle gently as you pass beneath their limbs. The cool, scented air is spotlighted with sunshine. Leaves crunch underfoot. It's an encounter that sticks to your senses.

The season's golden performers can be found along the national forest trails neighboring Durango. To learn the current color status and recommended aspen-canopied trails, contact Durango's National Forest Service office at 701 Camino del Rio, (970) 247-4874.

For a heightened awareness of the aspen glory, it may be helpful to know that the greens, yellows and reds exist in the leaves all year. Throughout the summer they are camouflaged by chlorophyll, the tree's green food producer. Changes in the amount of daylight and cooling temperatures cause the chlorophyll to slow its production, allowing other colors to make a final, glorious display.

Temperature and moisture are key factors influencing color changes. A warm, dry fall promises a late color display. A cool, rainy autumn brings on an early display. Colors generally peak in mid-to-late September. When high elevation trees have lost their golden tresses, look to lower elevations where the season's yellow blush is making its first appearance.

In the fall, aspen forests appear as several large families splashing their distinctive color across the slope. Growing in clusters and sharing the same root system, these members of the willow family are capable of duplicating themselves for thousands of years. Individually, aspens grow vigorously for 50 years.

While walking in an aspen forest,

Gold-shimmering aspens illuminate the forest along Lime Creek Road.

consider it a sanctuary of biological diversity, balanced so precisely that your presence must be temporary and traceless.

The following suggestions may make your visit more meaningful:

Discover the forest's natural serenity while standing silent amidst the symmetry of an aspen grove.

Tune in to the different rhythms whispering from each aspen glen.

Take time to witness the panoramas at your feet as well as those in limbs overhead. An anthill can be as awesome as an aspen-cloaked summit.

Introduce yourself to different aspen families or clones clustered in one large grove. Look for a family's subtle though distinguishing characteristics in trunk shape, bark whiteness and texture, leaf coloring and shape.

Examine aspen trunks for the gouged scars made by deer or elk antler rubs. Elk nibblings are distinguished by their two-tooth scars in horizontal rows. Blackened gouges show the tree's healing capacity. Recent damage shows the light green inner bark – cambium, a favorite late-winter forage for elk and deer.

Smell the bark or an armful of leaves. Unearth a handful of loose, dark mulch. Discover its fragrance and texture.

Above all, consider a fall hike a vitamin for your soul, an enriching dose of joy before winter chills the spirit.

Rodeo riders await their turn in one of three roughstock events: Bareback Bronc Riding, Saddle Bronc and Bull Riding. Little wonder professional rodeo is second only to baseball as the largest spectator sport in this country.

●

Internationally known musicians, dancers and actors are among the performing artists hosted at Fort Lewis College's Community Concert Hall.

Photo: ©Christopher Marona,1998

COWBOYS TO CONCERTOS

Art spans the cowboy-to-concerto spectrum in Durango. Here, an evening's entertainment might be listening to Bar-D Wranglers present their famous Old West Stage Show under a star-lit canopy or watching the internationally acclaimed Balleto di Toscano perform at Fort Lewis College's Community Concert Hall or simply browsing the dozen or more art galleries along Main and Second avenues.

A pulse on Durango's art beat is found at the Durango Art Center. Committed since 1966 to advancing the arts for the individual and the community, the nonprofit organization now has a permanent home on Second Avenue in downtown Durango. The former auto shop and dealership features a large gallery for displaying regional and traveling exhibits. The 17,000-square-foot building includes an interactive children's museum, a 250-seat theatre, a teaching studio, a conference room, additional office space and a gallery shop selling affordable local and international folk art. Acting as the local arts council, DAC helps support such annual events as the 11-day festival of classical Music in the Mountains at Purgatory Resort, the Bluegrass Meltdown each spring and the Durango Choral Society's Christmas Concert. Children's After-School

Theatre (C.A.S.T.) and the Arts Force, both extensions of DAC, offer professional training in the arts to the community's youth.

Another pulse point on the arts in Durango is the college's Community Concert Hall. Artists, be they cowboy singer Ian Thompson; or pianist Barry Douglas, winner of the Tchaikovsky Music Award; or members of the Central City

Since 1968 the Bar-D Wranglers have serenaded and told jokes to nearly 900 guests nightly during the summer's dinner shows.

Opera, are among the performers experiencing sold-out shows and standing ovations in this 612-seat building. Designed to mimic Carnegie Hall's acoustics, the concert hall is the first of three buildings in the Cultural Arts Complex at FLC.

Actors and actresses perform plays from Shakespeare to vaudeville on many stages

in town. The Durango Repertory Theatre, established in 1979, produces six shows a year, creating local talent for the town's ever-evolving stage companies. Drama departments at both the high school and college produce award-winning plays and musicals, while young actors land roles in Durango Lively Arts productions. Time magazine rated the Diamond Circle Melodrama at the Strater Hotel "one of the top three melodramas in the country."

Celebrating western heritage, the Durango Cowboy Gathering brings local and nationally known cowpokes to share their poems and songs during the town's annual fall event. Pro-rodeo shows throughout the summer and the four-day mid-summer Fiesta Days highlight the fun of cowboy life. Throughout the year, the town's dozen or more galleries showcase artists whose paintings and sculptures embody the Southwest, with Toh-Atin Gallery housing the world's foremost collection of Navajo weavings.

Rare is a stage empty, a gallery wall blank or a concert hall quiet in Durango – thanks to the town's network of organizations committed to art. Rated #4 in the 100 Best Small Art Towns in America (John Muir Publication, 1997), Durango is #1 according to the town's enthusiastic audiences and growing art community.

Climber ascends X-Rock, Durango's prime climbing site, located at the north end of town. Local guides offer climbing lessons here.

•

Climber checks ropes before ascending the pinnacle at X-Rock.

PLENTY OF PRACTICE PITCHES

Climbers tend to gear up in Durango before tackling some of the state's more challenging peaks in the Needles. They're drawn to Durango's collections of sandstone outcrops, where beginning to expert climbers find a plethora of walls to scale.

X-Rock, the best known of Durango's climb sites, names the rock located about six blocks north of 32nd Street. Two dozen or more routes thread this haven of sandstone boulders and cliffs. X-Rock itself and the 80-foot high cliff face with its namesake deeply carved across it, is a beginner's rock lined with an abundance of easy-to-moderate routes. The Boxcar, a 15-foot tall boulder below X-Rock, offers climbers overhangs and a vertical face with numerous holds – ideal features for rehearsing many climbing maneuvers.

X-Rock was first recognized as a climbing site in the late 1950s when only a few veterans of the World War II Mountain Troops practiced their training in nearby peaks. Dolph Kuss, Durango's first recreational program director and a leading local innovator in outdoor adventures, searched instead for the town's convenient climbs. His first venture brought him to what is now called X-Rock. After repeatedly clearing oak from the rock, he and his climbing companion, Ed Pacheco, hand drilled a hole at the rock's summit. They used a small army stove to melt lead then poured the hot metal in the hole to secure a bolt. From that same bolt climbers continue to hang safely suspended while rappelling the face of X-Rock.

East Animas, a climbing area named for its location on the east side of the

Carabineers, often clusters of them, are necessary equipment for climbers at most sites.

Animas River, is known for its variety of ascents on the 175-foot tall cliffs. Face, pitch and multi-pitch climbs done here require hands and feet only (plus brains and brawn) with a rope used for protection. Most of the area's free climbs are rated challenging.

Access to East Animas, sometimes called the Watch Crystal, is via Main Avenue, turning east on 32nd Street all the way to County Road 250, then turning left. A pull-out 3.5 miles from this intersection sits directly below the cliffs.

Turtle Lake Boulder Area lures locals who practice their moves on a collection of 15-foot high rocks. A scrub oak forest nearly masks this climbing site that is located across from a privately owned lake, northwest of town. To get there, turn west on 25th Street off Main Avenue, following it 2.9 miles to a fork. Take a sharp right and continue 1.1 miles to the pullout.

The most challenging and newest of Durango's climbing destinations is the Golf Wall, located north of Tamarron Resort on U. S. Highway 550. Only experienced lead climbers, adept at a gymnastic approach, ascend the "5.10" site's routes bolted with hardware.

Climbers in Durango, visitors and residents alike, remain a close-knit group, bonded by sunshine and a commitment to preserving another slice of the town's natural attractions.

Pack of men's pro racers begins the 5,500-foot ascent up U.S. Highway 550, the race course for the Iron Horse Bicycle Classic.

GETTING IN GEAR

It began as a contest between two brothers – young Tom Mayer, a bicyclist, and older brother Jim, a train engineer. Every day when the train to Silverton steamed past their home, Jim would blow the engine's whistle, and Tom would hop on his ten-speed and power-pedal 50 miles over two mountain passes, trying to beat his brother in the iron horse.

One day in 1971, as Jim pulled the train up to Silverton's station, there sat his 16-year-old kid brother, smiling and sweating. The next year, with the help of a neighbor Ed Zink, 36 cyclists joined their contest. They called it the Iron Horse Bicycle Race.

Today, world-class cyclists are among the 2,000 entrants competing in the Iron Horse Bicycle Classic, one of the biggest bike races held in the United States. Scheduled for Memorial Day weekend, the multi-classed event has grown to be one of the "oldest and most complex, sophisticated races," says Zink, the event's continuous, propelling force.

The grueling 47-mile, 5,500-feet climb to Silverton begins at 7 a.m., when the pro and men's senior classes leave from their starting gate two miles north of town. In 10-minute intervals, an additional 500 or more competitors join the race.

Meanwhile, hundreds of "Half Century Tour" riders position themselves for the ceremonial start of the race in downtown Durango. They peddle out of town as the coal-fired engine of the D&SNGRR train blasts its mournful call.

When the 1800s locomotive steams into Silverton 3-1/2 hours later, several racers will be there already to welcome it. The winner, jubilant with a score of 2 hours or

Lycra-clad cyclists start the Iron Horse Half Century tour as the D&SNGRR begins its 45-mile climb to Silverton.

less, will be milling around with fellow riders, all talking about ways they could have shaved seconds from their time. Only elite riders make it in 2 to 2-1/2 hours. Every year riders complete the race in 3 - 5 hours.

What's astounding is that while the remaining thousand cyclists try for a winning time or simply making it to Silverton, two-way vehicle traffic is interrupted only briefly on the race course – U. S. Highway 550. Precision scheduling such as this is credited to Zink and his crew of 100 or more dedicated volunteers. It also reflects the community's concern for the safety of the cyclists and motorists by focusing their spectating to the race's start.

Zink's crew is equally adept during the mountain bike events held on Sunday and Monday. Fat-tire bikes take to the slopes of Durango's Chapman Hill, where Zink's team coordinates the NORBA - National Off-Road Bicycle Association sanctioned dual slalom races and a dozen or more classes of cross-country events. Throughout the weekend they oversee scores of runners, swimmers, kids and cops competing in a variety of events.

The Iron Horse is the nation's biggest and oldest, continuously run bike race. In Durango, it's the peak event of the town's century-old sport, begun in the 1890s with the Durango Wheel Club (see page 62).

Mountain bikers compete in national and regional events held in Durango yearly.

Photo: ©Paul Ambrose, 1998

Cyclists ride the lift at Purgatory where miles of marked trails line the terrain. Some pedal directly to the course used during the 1990 World Mountain Bike Championship.

FIRSTS IN FAT TIRES

Firsts come naturally to the cycling scene in Durango. During the 1984 Iron Horse Classic, the town was first to host the only staged event in the U. S. that included both mountain bike and road races. Two years later, Ed Zink and the Iron Horse Classic organization successfully hosted Durango's first national mountain bike event. The following year, officials of the National Mountain Bike Championships asked for a repeat performance. By then, word of the varied terrain and skilled race organizers based here quickly spread. In 1990, Durango became the host city for the first officially sanctioned World Mountain Bike Championships.

Durango set the character and quality of the first world-class event by which future races would be measured. Zink and his committee of bike race volunteers, in keeping with their standard of excellence and environmental awareness, helped establish the nation's first state-wide symposium on mountain biking. A key session during the symposium pulled together a first-ever committee consisting of top people in the biking industry, sports media, race competitors and government land managers. Their discussion of the issues, challenges and opportunities inherent in this rapidly growing sport resulted in the first statewide mountain biking advisory committee.

Most notable among Durango's firsts is its resident cycling set. Ned Overend holds the lion's share of winnings as the NORBA champion in several world and national events including a European championship. Among his 20 or more award-winning, peddle-pumping compadres are Greg Herbold and John Tomac, both earners of sizable portions of the championship titles. Herbold holds the distinction of being the first officially recognized downhill mountain bike champion.

Durangoans Ruthie Matthes and Missy Giove reign as top female bikers in international events. Competing five times in the prestigious Tour de France, which qualifies only 200 racers world-wide, is Durangoan Bob Roll.

Durango's Fort Lewis College Cycling Team recently won three out of four National Collegiate Cycling Association championships. It only follows that nearly half of the 36-member U. S. team for the 1992 World Mountain Bike Championship in Canada consisted of Durangoans. Thus far, one-third of all world champion mountain bikers ever crowned call Durango their home.

Durango's bicycling event season begins in May with the ever-popular Iron Horse Bicycle Classic. Ride the Rockies peddles through every three years or so, and another national event is hosted here on a tri-annual basis. The Century Classic and Tour of the San Juans are scheduled for fall color rides, with Durango riders closing the cycling season in October at Farmington, New Mexico's Road Apple Rally. Bicycling events account for a whopping 60,000 visitor days in Durango, a town that many cyclists consider the Rocky Mountain capital for the sport.

A mud-caked mountain bike, evidence of the toll this grueling sport takes on both machine and rider.

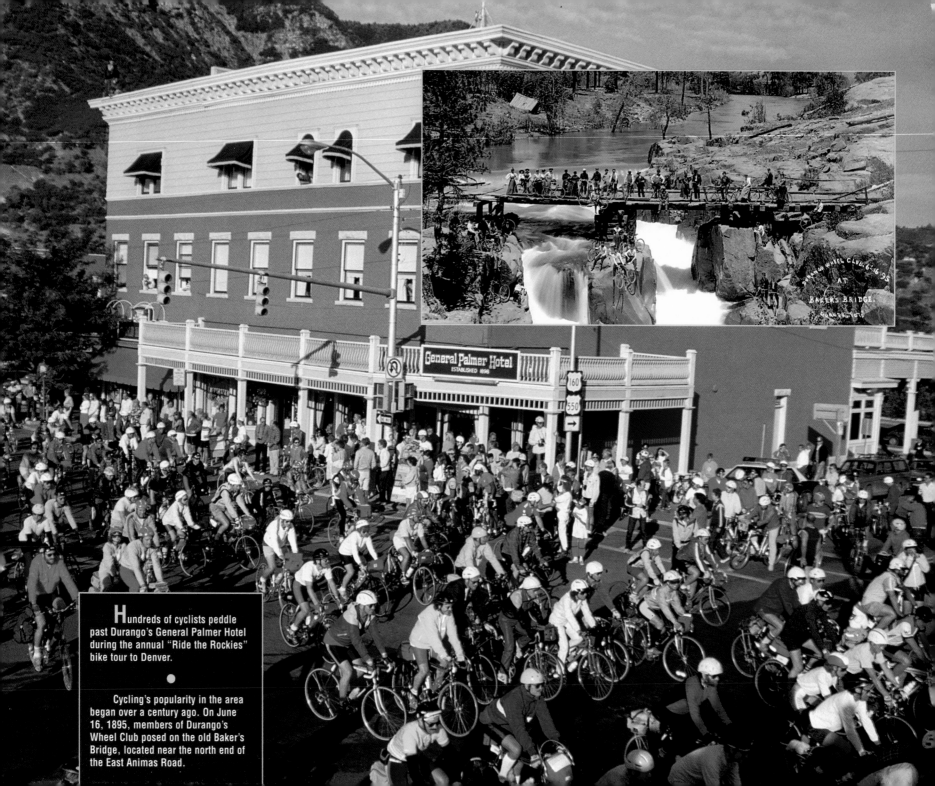

Within the photograph, the following text labels appear:

General Palmer Hotel
ESTABLISHED 1898

160
550

Hundreds of cyclists peddle past Durango's General Palmer Hotel during the annual "Ride the Rockies" bike tour to Denver.

●

Cycling's popularity in the area began over a century ago. On June 16, 1895, members of Durango's Wheel Club posed on the old Baker's Bridge, located near the north end of the East Animas Road.

DURANGO WHEEL CLUB 6-16-'95
AT
BAKERS BRIDGE.

CRUISING AND CLIMBING

For some, watching mud-splashed bikers maneuver their wheels down near vertical terrain is only half the fun. Most bikers would rather just be "doing it." And they'd prefer to stay out of the mud.

The Animas River Trail, a 12-mile hard-surface path beginning at the playground near 32nd Street and East Second Avenue, provides an easy tour of the city. Construction on the trail each year brings it closer to becoming free of street crossings and extending south to Escalante Middle School. The Animas Valley Loop, 30-mile, relatively flat route, passes the older ranches flanking the Animas River. It begins on County Road 250, the east end of 32nd Street, heading north to Trimble Lane or farther to the famous Baker's Bridge. Cross the river and U. S. 550 at either of these points to meet the return route, County Road 203. From Baker's Bridge, one must travel on U. S. 550 to the start of C. R. 203 about 5 miles south. Caution is advised on this busy section of roadway for all riders.

Another easy country ride begins in Bayfield on County Road 501 that gently rises on the road paralleling Vallecito Reservoir. This 19-mile excursion rolls along the Los Pinos River Valley, climbing 800 feet.

Century ride fans peddle to Dolores via the wide-shouldered U. S. Highway 160 to Mancos, where Highway 184 climbs to Summit Reservoir at mile 37. At the intersection of highways 184 and 145, they head south (left) to Cortez for the final 45-mile return trip east on U. S. Highway 160.

One of the most scenic and kind-to-the-quads rides is the 11-mile, aspen-canopied Old Lime Creek Road. Its southern end is located just two miles north of Purgatory. Mountain bikes are a necessity for this original "Old Highway from

Competitors peddle U.S. Highway 550, the race course for the Iron Horse Bicycle Classic. An estimated 60,000 visitor-days are attributed to Durango's season of bicycling events.

Durango." Those new to mountain biking or with time constraints start at the south end and ride the three miles to the lily-covered beaver ponds. A beautiful hike to Potato Lake begins here. Old Lime Creek's north end begins about 3 miles north of Coal Bank Pass. A shuttle vehicle left at the road's south end makes for an easy two-hour trip.

The Purgatory Ski Area is another arena for mountain bikers. While zealots prefer peddling to the top, its chairlift provides easy access to a web of alpine trails, each one rated according to difficulty. Mountain bike experts like testing their skills on the course set up for the 1990 World Mountain Bike Championship. Trail maps and further information may be found at the base area.

Hermosa Creek Trail, starting west of Purgatory on National Forest Road 578, features a challenging, 15-mile descent through dense tree stands and twice over streambeds.

Durango provides bicycle access to several points along the Colorado Trail, the 470-mile back-country route between Durango and Denver. Detours are provided around the bicycle-restricted wilderness areas. See The Colorado Trail book for details.

Bike tours to mining camps or ancient Indian ruins describe the range of options mountain bikers discover in Durango. Several local shops offer bike rentals, equipment, lunches, tour leaders and even a bike rack for your car.

For more information on area trails, see the booklet entitled "Bicycle Routes on Public Lands of Southwest Colorado," available at many sporting goods stores in the area.

Maureen Keilty, a Durangoan since 1976, writes about the Southwest's people and places for magazines and newspapers. She is author of Best Hikes with Children in Colorado (*The Mountaineers, 1991, 1998*) and Best Hikes with Children in Utah (*1993*).

Since the mid-70s Dan Peha has been creating photographic images of the Southwest for books, magazines and calendars. His photographs illustrated Maureen's books and many of her articles.

Maureen and Dan are currently introducing their young son, Niko, to the shoes seen on the back cover.